The Prepper's Urban Survival Guide to Los Angeles: A Plan to Escape, Survive, and Protect Your Family From Any Disaster

By Yoni Binstock

Disclaimer
All the material contained in this book is provided for educational and informational purposes only. No responsibility can be taken for any results or outcomes resulting from the use of this material.

While every attempt has been made to provide information that is both accurate and effective, the author does not assume any responsibility for the accuracy or use/misuse of this information.

Table of Contents

Introduction

One of my earliest childhood memories happened on Jan 17, 1994 at 4:30 am when I was around three or four years old living in Los Angeles. The 1994 Northridge earthquake had 6.7 magnitude record and ended in 57 deaths, with more than 8,700 injured and between $13 and $40 billion in property damages.

It shook the house so hard that the TV fell off the stand and the power went out. It probably only lasted a few minutes, but as a young child, it seemed like an eternity. And I was completely confused as to what had happened. The fact that my entire world could be so shaken up by natural forces was beyond my comprehension.

Since that fateful event, I have been interested in what happens during disasters and how people cope with disastrous events. Whenever a hurricane or a tornado ravaged a city, I was always interested in how people managed during these terrible events.

Many years later as a young adult, I became a volunteer EMT and joined the Los Angeles CERT (Community Emergency Response Team). It was important to me to have the skills and knowledge to protect myself and my family if a disaster struck my home.

When I was in training for the CERT-LA, I learned a very important lesson that stuck with me. During a city-wide emergency, you need to take care of yourself, and you should not expect emergency services to be able to provide for you. In many cases, they will be so busy attending to emergencies that there will be no guarantee that you will receive assistance. You, alone, are responsible for your well-being, and you need to take the necessary actions to prepare for any disaster.

While the world has become relatively safer over the past several centuries, life is still chaotic and unpredictable. Disasters, either man-made or natural, can strike in any city, at any time. Recently, shootings, explosions, coups, food-shortages, rioting, have all become uncomfortably common. No matter what city or what neighborhood you live in, terrible events can happen there and it is my goal after this book to continue writing other urban survival books for other cities around the world.

In Los Angeles, disasters such as flooding, earthquakes, wildfires, civil unrest, and terrorist related activities are all distinct possibilities. On the bright side, you don't need to worry about tornadoes or hurricanes. In this book, there are unique tips, instructions, and resources for Los Angeles disasters that will help you prepare for any scenario.

About the Book

This book is for anyone that is interested in learning more about how to stay safe and possibly escape the city following a disaster in Los Angeles. With the information from this guide, you'll know what to do to protect yourself and your family in a range of different emergency circumstances. You've already taken a great first step by purchasing this book. I would recommend reviewing the material once a year and always having it on your Kindle, so if a disaster strikes, you'll have all of the essential information at your fingertips.

In this book, we'll first go over the history of disasters in Los Angeles County, what services and plans exist for residents of the city, and other pertinent information regarding the area. The next chapter will detail everything you need to know about surviving a disaster. We'll cover subjects like how to prepare for a wide range of disasters, government emergency plans, and how to stay safe. The third chapter focuses on escaping the city including when you should go, avenues for getting out of the city, and what to bring with you. The chapter following will cover everything else you need to know about LA disasters including how to do a dry run, the importance of communities, and what psychological stresses you might face during a disaster. And then to wrap it all up, I give you a list of resources, social media accounts to follow for news, and more information on the Los Angeles emergency system.

Most excitedly, I've had the distinct pleasure of interviewing people involved with the LA disaster preparation and "prepper"/ emergency preparedness experts . Their answers offer insights you will not find anywhere else.

I encourage you to visit our website and sign up for our newsletter where we'll send out helpful suggestions on how to prepare for any disaster. www.urbanprepperguide.com

Follow us on social media
Google Plus: https://plus.google.com/102271917180581870090
Twitter: https://twitter.com/CityPrepperPlan
Facebook: https://www.facebook.com/The-Preppers-Urban-Survival-Guide-140050986438508/

Los Angeles and Disasters

A History of Disasters in Los Angeles

"Those who cannot learn from history are doomed to repeat it." - George Santayana

Earthquakes

On January 9, 1857, the greatest Southern California earthquake in modern history, the Fort Tejon Earthquake, measuring 8.0 on the Richter scale, shook the present-day communities of Wrightwood and Palmdale. Fortunately, Southern California was sparsely populated at the time, so there was minimal damage and loss of life. If it were to happen today, the damage would easily run into billions of dollars, and the loss of life would be beyond tragic.

On March 10, 1933, a magnitude 6.4 earthquake hit the Newport-Inglewood Fault, causing extensive damage in Long Beach and its neighboring communities. The earthquake led to more than $50 million in property damage and 120 deaths.

Recent earthquakes include: The San Fernando Earthquake on February 9, 1971 which caused more than $500 million in damage and 65 deaths, the 5.9 Whittier Narrows Earthquake which struck on October 1, 1987 causing eight deaths and $358 million in property damage, the 5.8 Sierra Madre Earthquake on June 28, 1991 resulting about $40 million in property damage and two deaths, and the 6.7 Northridge Earthquake which struck on January 17, 1994 causing 57 deaths, 20,000 homeless, and $30 billion in property damage.

Wildfires

Although Los Angeles is globally known as a sprawling concrete landscape, thousands of residents live in the hills of the Angeles National Forest and the Santa Monica Mountains National Recreational Area. Since 1927, 24 wildland fires have caused the loss of 1,502 homes and five fatalities.

Only recently, on July 22nd, 2016, a wildfire in the Santa Clarita Valley area (20 miles from downtown Los Angeles) has grown to more than 40,000 acres. A cloud of smoke blanketed much of Los Angeles, prompting the South Coast Air Quality Management District to issue a smoke advisory, especially for those who had respiratory problems. Luckily, only 18 homes were destroyed and no reported deaths.

Storms and Floods

Because Los Angeles County contains some of the steepest and most erosive mountains in the world (the San Gabriels), there is significant potential for floods and mudslides. In 1914, a storm caused more than 19 inches of rain to fall in the San Gabriel Mountains, producing floods causing $10 million in damages. On March 12, 1928, the St. Francis Dam broke just before midnight taking the lives of 600 residents as the water washed out with tremendous force into the Pacific Ocean.

In 1938, floods caused $70 million in damage and 115 deaths. From that disaster, work soon began on the Los Angeles River, the concrete channel that winds around the city preventing storm water overflow.

Heat Wave

In July of 2006, there were several days where the temperature stayed above 100 degrees F. The death toll across California was estimated to be above 163 persons (mainly elderly residents), as coroners had trouble processing the high volume.

Civil Disorder

Significant events of civil unrest are uncommon in the greater Los Angeles Area but have occurred twice in recent history. Six days of rioting began on August 11, 1965, leading to

34 deaths and 856 injured. The second time was after a jury, on April 29, 1992, acquitted four LAPD officers in the Rodney King trial, which led to the partial collapse in civil order, resulting in 58 deaths.

After the fatal shooting of Michael Brown on August 9th, 2014, by white police officer Darren Wilson in Ferguson, Missouri, protests and riots broke throughout the city. The police quickly issued a curfew and deployed riot control units. In just a few days, the people of Ferguson had their lives turned inside out as swat teams, looting, tear gas, rubber bullets, automatic weapons, flash grenades, smoke bombs, Molotov cocktails, members of the press being arrested, armored trucks, the national guard became part of their town. This pattern of police shooting, demonstrations, police crackdown, and riots repeated in cities like Cleveland, Milwaukee, Baton Rouge, and several others.

Important Information Regarding Los Angeles:

Tip the world over on its side and everything loose will land in Los Angeles. Frank Lloyd Wright

Stats
Population: ~4,000,000 people
Area: 503 mi²
Density: 8,282/sq mi
Police personnel to population: 3.3 / 100
Homicide rate: 7 / 100,000
Gangs: 450 active gangs with over 45,000 members
Number of grocery stores: 2,084
Median age: 31.6 years old
Persons under 5 years old: 6.2%
Persons above 65 years old: 14.9%
Persons with a disability: 8.5%
Pet dog to population: 19.9%
Pet cat to population: 13%
Households at high or extreme risk to wildfires: 1,989,100
People in nursing facilities/skilled-nursing facilities: 13,845
People in local jails and other municipal confinement facilities: 7,557
People in emergency and transitional shelters for people experiencing homelessness: 6,069
People in mental (psychiatric) hospitals and psychiatric units in other hospitals: 147
Chance of having a magnitude 6.7 or larger earthquake within the next 30 years: 99%

The Los Angeles County's Plan of Action

To best prepare for any emergency, it's best to know in detail what the city government is going to do and how it will affect you. Because of Los Angeles' history with natural disasters, the city has a relatively robust and in-depth emergency plan. This section helps you understand how the city and county will react to a variety of different emergencies.

According to the Los Angeles County Operational Area Emergency Response Plan (ERP), the Los Angeles County Operational Area is the main point of logistics and communication for all other agencies. The Sheriff, who acts as the Director of Emergency Operations, coordinates the County's and/or Operational Area's disaster response efforts.

Connect straight to the relevant sources of information below. This is where the county gets their information regarding disasters and emergencies.
• University of California Seismological Observatory, Berkeley
• California Institute of Technology, Pasadena
• Water Resources Department
• OES Regional Offices
• Federal/State/Local agencies
• Honolulu Observatory
• The National Weather Service

When a city wide disaster strikes, the Emergency Operations Center (EOC) is the focal point for coordination of the City's emergency planning, training, response and recovery efforts. This is the place that looks pretty much like a NASA launch room, the one you see in every movie that involves a global disaster.

To be ready for any disaster, the EOC is well prepared with assets including:
• 30-foot setback from the street
• Perimeter fencing
• Blast-resistant exterior surfaces
• Video surveillance system
• 24-hour on-site guards
• Access to NC4, NOAA weather information, Caltech seismic event information, the LA County EMIS Network, and the State of California's Operational Area Satellite Information System and Response Information.
• Emergency backup generators
• Centralized uninterrupted power source
• Reserve water and sewage storage tanks
• Redundant heating/ventilation/air conditioning systems

Agency Roles

During emergencies, some government agencies continue to operate in their normal capacity, but also may take on additional roles.

The Department of Animal Care and Control offers emergency animal housing at its shelters and patrols disaster areas to rescue domestic animals displaced by catastrophic events. Depending on the severity of the emergency, the Department may also set up temporary emergency animal shelters.

The Coroner is responsible for activating the Emergency Mortuary Response Plan, establishes a Death Notification Center, and Mass Fatality Collection Points.

The Department of Health Services (DHS) provides for the health and medical needs of the population of the Los Angeles area by coordinating private and public resources.

The Department of Public Social Services' (DPSS) In-Home Supportive Services (IHSS) Social Workers conducts health and welfare checks on high-risk disabled and elderly HISS recipients immediately following a disaster.

The Department of Public Works is responsible for making sure that the city's infrastructure is working properly and necessary repairs are being made. They update their road closure list here - http://dpw.lacounty.gov/roadclosures.

The City may ask any government employees to do work outside the normal scope of their duties as a Disaster Service Worker (DSW). All public employees in the State of California are considered potential Disaster Service Workers.

The Public Information Officers' (PIOs) role is to relay to the public with information about the emergency and instructions on what they should do. They will also be in communication with the media to provide accurate information about the extent of the emergency and response efforts, including programs and services for disaster victims. This vital information might include:

• What to do and what not to do
• Status of schools
• Status of hospitals
• First aid information
• Emergency telephone numbers
• Hazardous/contaminated/congested areas to avoid
• Road, bridge, freeway, conditions, and alternate routes
• Instructions/precautions about utility use, sanitation, how to turn off utilities
• Essential services available--hospitals, grocery stores, banks, pharmacies, etc.
• Weather hazards/public health risks
• Available State/Federal assistance.
• Curfews
• Disaster Application Center's opening dates/times
• Location of mass care/medical/coroner facilities, food, safe water
• Historical events of this nature
• Human interest stories
• Acts of heroism
• Historical value of property damaged/destroyed
• Prominence of those killed/injured
• During evacuations: routes, instructions (including what to do if your vehicle breaks down or

runs out of gas), arrangements for persons without transportation

Emergency Communication

Recently, the Emergency Alerting System (EAS) has been developed to provide the media the tools to disseminate emergency information, and enable the President, federal, state and local governments, to communicate with the public through commercial broadcast stations. If telephone services are not available, the Radio Amateur Civil Emergency Services (RACES) or Disaster Services Communications (DCS) becomes the default communication tool. To get the weather via radio, the National Weather Service (NWS) transmits continuous weather information on 162.40, 162.475 and 162.55 MHZ frequencies.

During an emergency, the following two warning systems may be activated by the county. The alerts will be sent via SMS, app notifications, tv, radio, and websites.

• Emergency Alerting System (EAS) is for upcoming events and conditions of concern to a significant segment of the population of Los Angeles County.
• Emergency News Network (ENN) allows messages to be sent via the State of California's Emergency Digital Information Service (EDIS) to the media, schools, and large businesses.

Priority Buildings
Below is a list of facilities that will be a high priority for emergency services and evacuation efforts and will, most likely, be safe. If you're in a location that you believe is unsafe, then you may want to move to a building that provides protection and relief.

• Fire Stations
• Sheriff/Police Stations
• County Hall of Administration
• County Emergency Operations Center
• Departmental Operations Centers
• Hospitals and Emergency Clinics
• Convalescent / Residential Care Facilities
• Blood Banks
• Public Works Yards
• City Halls

Additional Resources
For more information regarding government emergency plans, refer to any of the following
California Emergency Plan -
http://www.caloes.ca.gov/PlanningPreparednessSite/Documents/00%20SEP%207-01-09%20covrev%20(12).pdf
California Hazardous Materials Incident Contingency Plan -
http://www.caloes.ca.gov/FireRescueSite/Documents/HazMat%20Incident%20Contingency%20Plan%20-%20HMICP.pdf

California Law Enforcement Mutual Aid Plan -
http://www.caloes.ca.gov/LawEnforcementSite/Documents/1Blue%20Book.pdf
California Fire and Rescue Master Mutual Aid Plan -
http://www.caloes.ca.gov/FireRescueSite/Documents/CalOES%20-
%20Fire%20and%20Rescue%20-%20Mutual%20Aid%20Plan%20-%2020141201.pdf
SEMS Guidelines -
http://www.caloes.ca.gov/PlanningPreparednessSite/Documents/12%20SEMS%20Guidelines%
20Complete.pdf

Preparation for Different Types of Disasters

"In preparing for battle I have always found that plans are useless, but planning is indispensable."
-Dwight D. Eisenhower.

In an emergency, things can happen faster than you are able to process, which is why preparation and planning are so critical in survival. It takes away the cognitive load of developing a safe and thoughtful plan in a high-stress situation and instead only requires you to follow a checklist.

According to John Leach, a military survival instructor, in life-threatening situations, around 75% of people are so confused by the situation that they are unable to think clearly or plot their escape and just become mentally paralysed. When the Twin Towers were hit on 9/11, tragically many of the people in the buildings did not immediately evacuate. Those who eventually got out waited on average six minutes before moving to the exit, according to a study by the US National Institute of Standards and Technology. Unable to cope with what was happening to them, many either carried on as normal or stayed around to see what would happen. Mr. Leach continues saying that during a crisis, only 15% of people manage to remain calm and rational enough to make decisions that could save their lives. 10% freak out and hinder the survival chances of everyone else.

Having a plan is the most important thing you can to do prepare for a disaster. More so than buying a bug-out kit or installing a rain barrel, you need to have a written down plan and know what you and your family will do during a disaster.

Here are some things you can do to prepare for any emergency
• Install a backup power source
• Purchase a safe for your family valuables
• Install a rainwater collector
• Put together a first aid kit
• Put together a Bug-out bag / emergency supply cache
• Have 3 days worth of food and water
• Get to know your neighbors
• Drill a well or install a water storage tank (if you are able to)

Wildfires

Los Angeles County is home to the 650,000-acre Angeles National Forest and a large portion of the Santa Monica Mountains National Recreational Area. Thousands of homes are located in communities near these areas with a high risk of wildfires. The risk of you directly dealing with a wildfire will depend on where you live, but even fires that are miles in the hills can affect the air pollution at the Santa Monica Pier. No matter where you live in Los Angeles, wildfires can affect your home and your health.

Things to do to prepare
• Disengage the automatic garage door openers in the case of a power failure.
• Place your important records and documents inside your car.
• Keep at least 1/2-tank of fuel in your vehicle.
• Keep pet carriers handy.
• Sign up for alerts from your local fire department

During a Fire
• If you are inside a building, get out as quickly as possible. Before opening any door, touch the door/handle to determine if it is hot. Only if it is not hot, open it cautiously and be prepared to close it quickly if you see fire under the door. If the door is hot, find another way out and stay low to the ground to avoid smoke and fumes.
• Follow your building / home evacuation plan instructions and the directions from emergency personnel.
• Gather your family, pets and disaster supply kit and immediately leave your business or home.
• When you leave your home
    - Keep drapes and window coverings open
    - Close all interior doors and windows in your home
    - Keep interior lights on
    - Move combustible furniture away from windows and towards the center of the room
• Never park your vehicle in a traffic lane.
• Drive at a normal speed with your headlights on.
• Keep pets in carriers or on leashes.

After the Fire
• Do not return home before the area is declared safe by emergency personnel or local officials.
• Assess the damage to your home and check the utilities so that it's safe to return.

Storms, Floods, Landslides
Los Angeles County contains some pretty steep mountains, including the San Gabriels, reaching 10,000 feet above sea level. Below their steeply walled canyons lie large coastal plains and valleys with a very dense population center. When heavy rains come, water comes rushing down the mountain sides in fast moving streams and can possibly turn into a temporary flood. If you're in your vehicle, just two feet of water will carry your car away. Floods from a tsunami, from heavy rainfall, or a rupture in a dam can severely damage a city's infrastructure and hinder its transportation system. With the Los Angeles River helping with overflow, the risks of flooding in Los Angeles has been lessened, but not completely eliminated.

Before the Flood
• Assess the safety of your home in case of a flood or mudslide.
  - Are you near a creek?
  - Do you live above or below a steep hillside?
  - Do you have to drive over a creek or bridge to get to a main road?
• Clean gutters and drains around the house.
• If diversion of water or mud is necessary, plan to fill sandbags well before the rain starts. You can get sandbags at your local fire station. Take the time now to find out what fire station serves your area and learn the proper placement of sandbags.
• If you live in a hilly area, maintain the slopes on your property by using appropriate plantings, slope coverage, and drainage channels to reduce the risk of flooding.

During the Flood
• Look out for mudslides and adjust drainage to reduce mudslides.
• Do not cross rapidly flowing streams. Most streams will go down in a couple of hours, after it stops raining. Even a very shallow stream can knock a person off their feet.
• Check the drainage systems at your home and driveways.
• If caught in a slide or in a flood, move quickly out of the path of the debris flow and try to locate a stable and safe area. It can include a tree, a roof, or anything that will not be swept away.

After the Flood
• Check with the Department of Public Works at www.ladpw.org to find out what roads are damaged.
• Don't return to your flood-damaged home before the area is declared safe by emergency personnel.
• Check for injured or trapped individuals
• Check on neighbors who may need special assistance such as disabled persons, children, elderly, etc.
• Drive slowly and carefully as many roads may have mud, debris, holes, and washed-out areas.

Earthquakes
        Southern California has about 10,000 earthquakes each year, of those, 15-20 are greater than magnitude 4.0. As the most likely out of all the disasters reviewed by this book, preparing for earthquakes is a prudent thing to do. Earthquakes can range from being a mild inconvenience to tearing apart highways, toppling buildings, and breaking water lines. Unfortunately, there is no warning system for earthquakes, so there is nothing you can do to escape or be in a safe place when an earthquake strikes. This is why having a plan and being prepared is so important.

Before the Earthquake
• Identify safe spots in each room of your home. Find the sturdy tables, desks, and interior walls.
• Know your danger areas such as windows, mirrors, hanging objects, fireplaces, and tall, unsecured furniture.

• Conduct practice drills with your family and know the safest locations in your home.
• Decide where your family will reunite, if apart during an earthquake.
• Choose an out-of-state relative or friend to contact so that family and friends can know your status.
• Learn First Aid and CPR and put together a First Aid Kit.
• Secure major appliances as well as tall, heavy furniture, mirrors, and hanging plants.
• Learn how to shut off gas, water and electricity - it may be necessary during an earthquake.
• Keep breakables, heavy objects, and flammable or hazardous liquids such as pest sprays, cleaning products, paint cans in closed cabinets or on lower shelves.

During the Earthquake
• If indoors, stay there. Do not use the elevators and do not run to the exits.
•Stand in a corner away from a window or get under a desk or table.
•Watch out for falling plaster and ceiling tiles. Stay under a sturdy cover (such as a table) until the shaking stops.
•Stay away from bookcases, file cabinets, heavy mirrors, hanging plants and other heavy objects that could fall.
• If driving, pull over to the side of the road and stop. Stay in your car until the shaking is over and avoid areas around power lines.
• If outdoors, get to an open area away from trees, buildings, and power lines.
• Contrary to popular belief, being in doorway **is not** the safest place to be during the shaking.

After the Earthquake
• Stay calm
•If you become stuck under debris, try to move as little as possible so you don't loosen any heavy objects or stir up dust. Tap on a pipe, wall, or other hard object to attract rescuers. Shout only as a last resort. Cover your nose and mouth with any available cloth to avoid inhaling dust.
• Do not use the telephone unless there is an immediate, life-threatening emergency.
• Stay away from downed power lines.
• If it is safe and you know how to, check for gas and water leaks, and broken electrical wiring or sewage lines.
• If there is damage to your gas line, turn the utility off at the source and immediately report gas leaks to the utility company.
• If you are able and willing, and the area is safe, look around for anybody who needs medical attention.
• Do not attempt to relight the gas pilot unless your gas line has been inspected.
• Turn on your portable radio, check social media, and find news sources for instructions and news reports.
• Cooperate fully with public safety officials and follow their instructions.
• Do not use your vehicle unless there is an emergency.
• Be prepared for aftershocks.
• If you evacuate, leave a message on your door telling family members and others where you can be found.

Disease Outbreak

An outbreak can happen when a disease is new to a community, been absent for a long time, or has a population uniquely vulnerable to infection. The most serious outbreaks occur when people have little or no immunity, and there is no vaccine to prevent or medication to treat the illness. A large outbreak that sweeps across the nation and world is called a "pandemic." The disease may spread, cause serious illness and potentially impact daily community life. Wherever and whenever a disease outbreak occurs, neighbors can help other neighbors through planning, preparedness, and concern for their community's health. Fortunately, nothing as serious as the 1918 Spanish Flu has occurred since, but diseases like SARS, MERS, H1N1, Ebola, Bird Flu, and Zika all could have been very deadly if not for the quick responses by the global health community. A global health pandemic is a pretty low risk event, but who knows what comes next in nature's lethal arsenal.

In an interview with Bill Gates and The Verge magazine, when asked what he feared the most his response was the risk of a lethal worldwide pandemic. He believes that recent diseases like Ebola has shown the limits of our health response capabilities and that the Spanish Flu killed many more people than WWI and WWII, but we still spend far more money on military defense, than pandemic defense.

Things you can do to prepare for a pandemic
• Store two weeks worth supply of food and water.
• Periodically check your regular prescription drugs to ensure a continuous supply
in your home.
• Have any nonprescription drugs and other health supplies on hand, including pain
relievers, stomach remedies, cough and cold medicines, vitamins, and fluids with electrolytes.
• Stay up to date for vaccines for yourself and your family members.
• Talk with family members and loved ones about how they would like to be cared for if they got sick.
• Volunteer with local groups to prepare and assist with emergency response.
• Wash your hands with warm water and soap before eating.

During a pandemic, here are some steps you can take
• Wash hands with soap and water frequently.
• Stay inside and away from other people as much as you possible can.
• Clean your home and dishware often.

Some items that you should get as soon as you can after a pandemic is announced:
• 5 gallons of liquid bleach per person (to make potable water)
• Safety goggles and/or a face shield
• Boxes of exam gloves
• Antibacterial Soap and/or Hand Wipes
• 50 heavy duty black large garbage bags and 100 ordinary kitchen trash bags per person
• 50 rolls of toilet paper per person
• 10 rolls of paper towels per person

• Water filtration and purification devices
• Medical masks

Terrorism

Devastating acts of terrorism in America and around the world have left many concerned about the possibility of future attacks in their own cities. Keeping in mind that you're more likely to be fatally crushed by furniture than killed by a terrorist, you can also be aware of your surroundings and be prepared for the worst.

Things to keep in mind
• Los Angeles County utilizes a Terrorism Early Warning (TEW) group to constantly assess terrorist threats and to keep authorities and the public updated.
•Terrorists are most likely to target high-value locations including military and civilian government facilities, international airports, large cities, high foot traffic spots, and well-known landmarks.
•Your local authorities will provide you with the most accurate information specific to an event in your area. Stay tuned to local radio, television, and social media for news and warnings.
• If you are advised by local officials to "shelter in place."
> - Remain inside your home or office and protect yourself there.
> - Close and lock all windows and exterior doors.
> - Turn off all fans, heating and air conditioning systems.
> - Close the fireplace damper. Get your disaster supplies kit, and make sure the radio is working.
> - Go to an interior room without windows that's above ground level.
> - In the case of a chemical threat, an above ground location is preferable because some chemicals are heavier than air, and may seep into basements even if the windows are closed.
> - Seal all cracks around the door and vents with duct tape.
> - Stay put until you are told all is safe or are told to evacuate.
• Local officials may call for evacuation in areas at great risk.

Explosions are the most common type of lethal terrorist attack. Explosions can be caused by an IED (improvised explosive device) made with items bought over the shelf triggered remotely, by using a car to get the explosives somewhere very quickly, or a person wearing a suicide vest who can easily blend into a crowd. Besides the raw power of the explosion, a victim may also be injured by debris, hear ringing in their ears, or have minimal visibility with dust in the air.

Tips on surviving an explosion
• If you sense that an explosion is a split second away, drop to the floor and lie flat on your stomach and cover your head and ears with your hands.
• After an explosion occurs, leave the bomb site as quickly as possible.
• Do not linger to retrieve personal belongings or to make a phone call.
• Help injured victims who may need assistance walking away from the site.

Especially in America, mass shootings have become tragically frequent in occurrence. In schools, movie theatres, military bases, nightclubs, in the streets, and so many other places, people have lost their lives when someone has had access to guns and wanted to cause damage.

Tips on Surviving a Shooting
• If you are in the open, and you hear/see someone shooting in the crowd, immediately seek cover and concealment by staying low, out of eyesight as quickly as possible.
• Take a few seconds to take stock of the event taking place.
• Find all the possible exits and head towards the one furthest away from the point of danger.
• If you are out of the area, contact medical or emergency personnel right away.
• If you are unable to exit the premises, try to find a room you can lock yourself in as well as other nearby persons. Bar the door with furniture, shut off the lights, and get away from the windows.

Tsunamis

Tsunamis are caused by earthquakes, volcanic eruptions, or massive undersea landslides that displace a large mass of water. From the focus point, waves travel outward in all directions. As the tsunami nears the coastline, it may grow significantly in height and tear into the shore, causing an enormous amount of destruction and loss of life.

Recent tsunamis include the 2004 Indian Ocean Tsunami that had a death toll of over 230,000 and resulted in $14 billion dollars in humanitarian aid, the 2011 Tohoku Earthquake and Tsunami which killed roughly 25,000 persons and led to the meltdown and disaster at the Fukushima Nuclear Power Plant.

According to a recent research study by UC Riverside and U.S. Geological Survey scientists, earthquakes off the coast of Los Angeles are more likely than previously thought and tsunami wave heights could approach as high as 20 feet in the Ventura Harbor. Especially for those in the Ventura and Oxnard neighborhoods which are low lying and by the coast, residents should prepare for the possibility of a tsunami.

Some notes about tsunamis
• People near the seashore during a strong earthquake should listen to a radio for a tsunami warning and be ready to evacuate at once to higher ground.
• If you are at the beach and you notice the water has pulled back, creating a vast expanse of exposed beach, this is a warning that a tsunami may be imminent.
• If you are at home at the time of the warning, calmly gather up your family and go to a designated evacuation site or to any safe place outside your evacuation zone.
• Obviously, but needs to be said, never go to the beach to watch for or to surf a tsunami wave.

Power Blackout

Power failure can be the result of a power station problem, damage to a power line, short circuit at a critical node, and now, possibly, from a hacker. Hospitals, various government buildings, telecommunications facilities, and other places where the use of power is critical often utilize emergency power generators that will last for the short term.

Imagine that you are not able to keep your food fresh, warm or cool your house, heat water or food, fill your car with gas, pump water in or out of your home, charge your electronic devices, light your home, get out of an elevator, or get cash out of an ATM. How quickly the power is restored will determine the severity of the impact, but even a few hours after a blackout, the city can quickly be put under a lot of stress pushing its resources to the limits.

On August 14, 2003, a software bug overloaded transmission lines that were disrupted by foliage, affected an estimated 10 million people in Ontario and 45 million people in eight U.S. states. Water systems in several cities lost pressure and several television and radio stations were knocked off for a few hours or for the entire time of the blackout. There were also sewage spills, rail-line knocked offline, closure of regional airports and factories, inoperable gas stations and refineries, and cellular communication disruption. Power came back to affected areas ranging from a few hours later to 2 days. Fortunately, power was restored relatively quickly, but sometimes I wonder what would have happened to the affected 50 million people, if it had taken just a few days longer.

Things to do to prepare for a blackout
• Store ready-to-eat foods that do not require refrigeration.
• Keep a portable hand cranked radio in your home.
• Know where your flashlights are, and have plenty of backup batteries.
• Keep plenty of water on hand.
• ATM machines often will not work during a power outage, so keep a small amount of cash set aside.
• Prepare non-digital entertainment options (such as cards, board games, etc).
• Know how to use the manual override of your electric garage door.

Things to do during a blackout
• Listen to your battery/hand crank powered radio for the latest news.
• Leave your refrigerator and freezer doors closed so the food remains as fresh as possible.
• Use flashlights for lighting. Candles can often be hazardous.
• Turn off electrical equipment that you were using when the power went out, except for one light turned on so you'll know when power has been restored.
• Do not run a generator inside your home or garage.
• Make sure that your pets have plenty of water to drink and food to eat.
• With your AC unit un-operational, open your windows and close the shades to keep it dark, but letting the breeze in. Also make sure to stay hydrated to avoid heat-related issues. This is especially relevant for Los Angeles.

Survival

A City's Worst Nightmare

Imagine this scenario. The city has been without power for 10 hours. Beginning as a mild inconvenience, it has turned into a city-wide nightmare. Car collisions keep on rising as traffic lights stop working. Frozen food is starting to go bad, and people are sweltering in the heat without the air conditioning. Police and emergency personnel are stretched to their limits, and there's no solution in sight.

Another 10 hours pass and the situation keeps on getting worse. Laptops and cellphones have depleted their batteries and without any way to charge them, communication and staying up to date has become more difficult. Bands of rioters and looters start taking to the streets and helping themselves to easy pickings, but avoid confrontation with the police. Statewide resources are being mobilized to the city, a state of emergency is called, and the national guard is put on alert.

Ten more hours and the city is starting to lose control. Backup generators of critical buildings are starting to fail and people are panicking. Those who had not left before are locked in by deadlocked traffic and are starting to run out of basic resources. FEMA and other national emergency organizations are brought in to assist.

In just 30 hours without power, the Los Angeles you knew is turned into a disaster zone. Social order has broken down, clean water and food has become scarce, and you're stuck in the city.

What would you do? How would you react to a situation like that? Are you ready to protect yourself and your family?

Those were the questions I asked myself and over a long time researching and talking to experts, I compiled this plan to survive in a city undergoing a disaster. Having a plan is going to ensure that you can keep your family safe in any emergency.

Your Emergency Plan

Once a year, you should discuss your emergency plan with your family, or anyone you may live with. Having everyone on the same page is going to lead to calm and rational choices made when stress could possibly take over. You may want to print the plan and have it on the fridge or in another easily visible location. This is especially important if a disaster strikes while you're separated from your family and are unable to contact them.

Here are some topics you should cover in your emergency plan.
• Identify the threats in your area.
• Set up meeting places outside your home and outside your neighborhood.
• Select your out-of-state contact.

• Organize your important documents in a place that is easily accessible.
• Know your evacuation routes including exits and alternate ways to leave home and Los Angeles.
• Know the location of utility shut-offs (water, gas, and electricity).
• Know the emergency policies of schools and adult-care centers.
• Organize and review your emergency supplies.
• Figure out your transportation options.
• Make special provisions for children, seniors, pets, people with disabilities, or people who are not native-English speakers.
• Schedule annual disaster drills.
• Discover the back streets, government buildings, and other important locations in your neighborhood.
• Store all emergency contact numbers (fire, police, ambulance, etc.) in multiple places that all family members know.
• Teach children how and when to call 911 or your local Emergency Medical Services number as well as important phone numbers to memorize and your home address.
• Enroll in First Aid and CPR classes.
• Keep a fire extinguisher in your home and show everyone how to use it.
• Replace stored water every three months and stored food every six months.
• Make an inventory and, ideally, videotape or photograph your valuables.
• Install smoke detectors on each level of the home and hallways near bedrooms. Check them each month and replace batteries when necessary.

Emergency Supplies

To be fully prepared for a disaster, you got to have the right emergency supplies. We'll go over a bug-out bag in another chapter, but in this section, I wanted to talk about what you should have in your home in case of an emergency. Remember, everyone will have a slightly different backup cache, suiting their specific needs and preferences.

Here is a list of things you should have in stock at all times in your home. You may also want to create a smaller version for your car.

• Prescription medications and eyeglasses
• Infant formula and diapers (if applicable)
• Important family documents such as copies of insurance policies, bank account records, I.D. cards and, in case of separation, photos of family members and pets for identification
• Cash
• Backpack
• Battery powered flashlight
• Cell phone charger
• Nutrition/protein bars
• Canned foods and juices (enough for 3-10 days)
• Eating Utensils
• Water (at least 1 gallon per person, per day)

- Household liquid bleach to treat drinking water
- Pet food and extra water for your pet (if applicable)
- Food for infants, elderly persons, or persons on special diets
- Moist towelettes
- First Aid Kit*
- Tools: whistle, duct tape, plastic sheeting, wrench or pliers to turn off utilities, work gloves, can opener, all purpose knife, etc
- Sleeping bag or warm blanket for each person
- Complete change of clothing, including a long-sleeved shirt, long pants, and sturdy shoes.
- Personal Hygiene Kit (includes shampoo/body wash, wash cloth, toothbrush and toothpaste, comb, deodorant, and sanitation supplies)
- Books, games, and puzzles for children
- Battery-operated radio
- Local maps
- List of emergency telephone numbers
- Pens, pencils, paper

*First Aid Kit should include all of these in addition to the supplies for your personal medical needs.
- Adhesive tapes
- Hydrogen peroxide
- 4x4 gauze pads
- Band-Aids (assortment of different sizes)
- Ice packs
- Triangular bandages
- Ace bandages
- Scissors
- Cotton balls/Q-tips/cotton applicators
- Tweezers
- Penlight
- Thermometer
- Safety pins and sewing needles/thread
- Optional: over-the-counter pain medication and digestive aid
- Anti-bacterial towelettes
- Blood-stopper compresses
- Burn ointment
- CPR shield
- Tribiotic ointment

Kids at School

If you have children, and they are at school during a disaster, principals or other school representatives will remain on site until all students have been picked up from school. If an earthquake or another disaster prevents parents or guardians from picking up students when school is over, students will be sheltered at the school. Schools have plans and resources for extended stays by keeping food and other supplies for students and staff onsite.

If a school must be evacuated due to a risk to the facilities or surrounding area, students will be evacuated by school bus or other means to another district school site. Parents and guardians will be notified through local radio station announcements about evacuations and transfer sites where they can pick the students up.

Water

One of the biggest challenges in any disaster that last longer than 24 hours is clean drinking water. A normally active person needs to drink at least two quarts of water each day. Children, nursing mothers, and others may need even more than that. Hot temperatures, not unknown in Los Angeles, can double the amount of water needed. To be best prepared, recycled self-stored water every six months and commercially bottled water every 12 months.

In an emergency, you can use water that is already in your water heater tank, plumbing, and in ice cubes. **Do not** use water from the reservoir tank of your toilet, pool, or jacuzzi.

One of the easiest ways to get clean drinking water is with bleach, which most people have in their home. Here are the ratios for purifying water with bleach. After adding the bleach, shake, or stir the water container. Let stand 30 minutes before drinking.
1 Quart (water): 4 Drops (bleach)
1 Gallon: 16 Drops
5 Gallons: 1 Teaspoon

Another source of water can be from your hot water heater. Turn off the power that heats the tank and let it cool. When you want water, place a container underneath and open the drain valve at the bottom of the tank.

Staying in the Know

When a disaster strikes, right after your safety is secured, the next important step is finding more information on what's going on. You'll want to use all of the tools that you have at your disposal including your phone, radio, tv, and computer. Prioritize official and government sources for reliable information, but utilize tools like twitter to get a real time account of what's happening in your city.

There are five emergency broadcast systems where you can stay up to date with all of that emergency information

1. The Emergency Alert System
Emergency information is broadcasted directly by the Los Angeles County Sheriff's Department. For emergency events and conditions of widespread concern, a broadcast message will be sent to the public via radio and television stations.

2. Alert LA County

Alert LA County is a Community Mass Notification System that will be used in emergencies to contact county residents and businesses through phone messages, text messages, and e-mail. To register your cell phone, voice over IP phone number and e-mail address go to www.lacounty.gov and click on the link to "Alert LA County".

4. Amateur Radio

Los Angeles County Disaster Communications Service (DCS) works with ham radio operators throughout the County to provide reliable emergency communications.

5. Websites

Websites like the National Weather Service, www.nws.noaa.gov, allow you to sign up for web feeds that are sent directly to your computer. For county updates after a disaster, go to www.lacounty.info. The LA County website will list shelter locations and other essential survival information. I would also recommend using websites like Twitter, Facebook, and other social media platforms to stay up to speed with what's going on.

Taking Care of Pets

During an emergency, you may have a furry friend that needs your protection. Nearly 30% of Los Angeles residents own a dog or a cat that can make managing disasters a bit more difficult. It's estimated that thousands of people refused to evacuate New Orleans in advance of Hurricane Katrina because they weren't willing to leave their dogs or cats behind and there were no shelters supporting animals. After some of those who weren't willing to leave their animals died and pictures of stranded dogs and cats were displayed to the american public, disaster management and relief organizations started to incorporate pets into their plans. On October 6, 2006 The Pets Evacuation and Transportation Standards Act (PETS) requires states that ask assistance from FEMA to accommodate pets and service animals in their plans for evacuating residents facing disasters.

Follow this checklist to make sure you have everything to care for your pet in a disaster.
• Name tags and phone numbers for collars and harnesses.
• Leashes, harnesses, gloves and carriers to transport pets safely and securely
• Water and food for 3-10 days.
• Supplies like bowls, cat litter, and pans, manual can opener, foil or plastic lids for cans
• 3-10 day supply of medications and medical records.
• Photos of your pets in case they get lost.
• Information on feeding schedules, medical conditions, behavior problems, and the name and number of your veterinarian in case you have to board your pets. Don't forget pet beds and toys!
• First Aid kit (including large/small bandages with elastic tape, scissors, tweezers, Q-tips, antibiotic ointment, saline eyewash, & hydrogen peroxide).

Disaster Strikes - What Do You Do?

When disaster strikes, you and your family may have injuries, be emotionally stressed, or have damage to your property. The most important thing to remember is not to panic and help those who need assistance.

• Only if needed, call emergency services, then locate and notify family members of your circumstances.
• Find a safe spot in your home or at a shelter and follow local safety instructions.
• Stay up to date with information coming from emergency providers and utility providers.
• Listen to emergency officials, either evacuate your home, stay put, or begin recovery steps.

Stuck in the City and Can't Get Out

If you find yourself unable to evacuate Los Angeles and the disaster scenario is not improving, you may be forced to survive for an unforeseen amount of time. Since this could be for 2 days or longer, you need to be prepared to deal with the indirect dangers associated with long-term city-wide disasters. There may be a FEMA or Red Cross camp to find shelter and safety or you may have to hole up in your home. If the roads are blocked and the city's infrastructure is damaged, the city very quickly can possibly run out of food, fuel, water, and other necessities.

Here are some other things to do when you're stuck in a Los Angeles unable to maintain law and order
• Reach out to your community and neighborhood
• Procure water and food as much as you can while remaining safe
• Ration your resources
• Barricade your home
• Create a couple areas in your home or on your property where you can safely hide food
• See if there are emergency shelters, camps, or facilities nearby
• Avoid leaving your home unless necessary and knowing you'll be able to return

Dealing with Other People

I believe, in large part due to movies, that we have a preconception that as soon as the proverbial shit hits the fan, we'll all go Mad Max overnight. Instead, according to John Drury at the University of Sussex and Steve Reicher at the University of St Andrews, in a study of 11 mass tragedies, they showed that group solidarity was more prevalent than selfishness. They believed that people's tendency to help each other during disasters increases the chances of survival for everyone. Working with other people who live nearby, sharing resources, and helping each other will dramatically improve your chances of surviving.

If security isn't being provided by city, state, or national forces, then gangs and looters will take advantage of that power vacuum and use that to their advantage. The safest thing for you to do is to avoid confrontation at all cost. Your safety and those of anyone you're traveling with comes first, before shelter, food, or water. Similarly, if someone is mugging you at gunpoint, even if there was a chance that you could take him out, the safe and right thing to do would be to give him anything he wants. By avoiding detection, fortifying your home, joining other individuals in groups, or finding government shelters, you can vastly reduce the risk of violence to your person.

Escape

Time to Hit the Road

The Greater Los Angeles Area has an estimated population of 18 million people and is known for having terrible traffic. Can you imagine what the 405 or the 101 would look like if the local government decides to issue an evacuation order,? In the best case scenario, traffic would be moving at a crawl, in the worsts, cars stuck in place for 24 hours or more. With limited supplies that can fit in a car and stuck between thousands of others in similar dire situation, you would be one of the worst places to be after a disaster. Emergency personnel are going to have a difficult time getting anywhere and the temperature on the freeways in Los Angeles are going to cause heat related issues very quickly.

Keeping all of that in mind, you're home can be in direct threat and it wouldn't be safe or prudent to not leave. This chapter is going to help you build an evacuation plan that will get you and your family out of Los Angeles quickly and safely.

Recent Evacuations

In recent history, there are two evacuations worth looking at. New Orleans during Hurricane Katrina and Houston during Hurricane Rita. In New Orleans, evacuation efforts were disorganized and enacted too late. Many people, including the elderly and disabled, died because of it. In Houston, people were stuck on the freeway, some for 24 hours. Many motorists could not find gas, food or a bathroom. A tragic incident during that evacuation was the death of 24 nursing home residents who died when their chartered bus caught fire and exploded.

Because of the percentage of car owners, the density of the city, and the limited amount of freeway space, there is no doubt that Los Angeles will struggle with a mass evacuation order. You will have to determine to either evacuate or stay put based on estimated traffic (current and future), government evacuation orders (or lack of them), risk of harm, and a safe destination.

The Evacuation Order

When the local government is considering an evacuation order, they have to balance moving people out of a dangerous area and having millions of people stuck on the roads. In an emergency situation, they may use three warnings to inform the public what to do. To reach out, they will use television broadcast, social media, FM/AM radio, and helicopters equipped with a PA system.

1) An Evacuation Warning or Voluntary Evacuation means that you need to be ready to leave your home and the area at a moment's notice. Gather your family, pets, bug-out bag, and

important paperwork and listen for instructions from emergency responders. If you have special limited mobility or medical needs, you should exit the area when an Evacuation Warning is issued.

2) An Evacuation Order or Mandatory Evacuation is a directive to leave your home or business immediately. Once you have left the area, you will not be able to return until the order has been lifted. An Evacuation Shelter may be set up by the Red Cross at the request of the County if an area must be evacuated for an extended amount of time. Local officials will announce the location for an evacuation shelter once the shelter is ready to accept evacuees. If you evacuate, remember to leave information on your house door, so others know where you are planning to go.

3) Shelter-in-Place means the best place to be safe is inside. If authorities advise you to shelter-in-place you should turn off your air-conditioner and fan units, seal the gaps around windows and doors, stay put, and listen for authorities to announce the threat is over. Let friends and loved ones know that you are staying at home. Prepare to evacuate on very short notice and listen for information, updates, instructions, or warnings.

When an evacuation order is given, the county emergency program will be responsible for coordinating all evacuation measures. Immediately, they will target evacuation routes and points to minimize congestion and provide transportation for buildings with a higher concentration of people. They will also do the following:
• Expedite the movement of people from hazardous areas.
• Institute measures to prevent unauthorized people from entering vacated areas.
• Provide for evacuation to appropriate PUPs (pick up point), EPs (evacuation point), and shelters.
• Provide adequate means of transportation for people with disabilities and without vehicles
• Control evacuation traffic.
• Anticipate and prepare for the needs of individuals with household pets, livestock, and service animals.
• Provide initial notification, ongoing information, and reentry communications to the public through the Joint Information Center (JIC).
• Ensure the safe reentry of evacuees.

In the case that you are without transportation or feel more safe with the authorities, then head to a crowded area with high importance. Government buildings, large office buildings, schools, religious buildings, hospitals are all places where priority will be high in evacuating people. Your first thought is going to be to jump your car and be the first out before an evacuation order is given. While it would be smart to hit the road right away, there are several considerations to be aware of while evacuating in your car that could leave you in more risk than staying put.

• Damage to the infrastructure or debris may prevent motor vehicles from traveling on the highway system or roadways.

• Following an earthquake incident, roads and bridges will likely require inspection following each significant aftershock causing delays.
• If the electricity is out, traffic signals will not be working, which would slow the motor vehicle evacuation process.
• If there is damage to gas pipelines, vehicles may not be able to get fuel.
• If there is no electricity, the fuel will not be able to be pumped.
• Communications networks for gas stations may be down and pay at-the-pump, credit, or debit transactions may be unavailable.

Evacuation Options

During an evacuation, it's important to plan for multiple options and routes. Try to find information about the route and mode of transport you plan on taking before you leave your home. Most likely, your first thought is going to get into your own car and get the hell out of Dodge City. But before heading out and potentially getting stuck on your own on the freeway, you might consider vehicles from schools, law enforcement, private shuttle, and charter bus companies that will be used to evacuate the public. By using these services, you will be protected by city emergency personnel. They will also know which routes are open, and the evacuation points to take people to. The downside is that you would have to wait for the order to be given.

Besides your own vehicle and government emergency services, there a few other ways to evacuate Los Angeles.

First is the rail system. Although constricted by its freedom of movement, it can move a lot of people quickly to relatively far distances. The three rail transport providers are the MTA, Metrolink, and Amtrak which all have procedures in place if there is an evacuation order.

Second, you can escape by sea. While limited by the amount of vessels and accessibility, aquatic vehicles deserve consideration for their freedom of movement. Options include ferry boats, tour boats, cruise ships, or sailing boats.

You may want to look into the Transportation Workers Identification Card (TWIC) and seamen credentials. Both are available to every American Citizen. You can acquire both of these credentials at Coast Guard Regional Exam Center (REC). The Coast Guard will take your fingerprints to conduct an FBI background check, ask you to fill out a few form, and in a few days you should get your credentials. The TWIC card is issued by the TSA and looks like a driver's license, allowing you into any port in the country. Before you head out to sea, make sure to have a handheld VHF radio. For around 100 dollars, a VHF will give you access to channel 16, the frequency of the Coast Guard, and the port's working channel. It will also pick up NOAA weather and emergency broadcasts as well as reports from vessels already out at sea. This is great to know exactly what the situation is at sea before you make your aquatic escape.

Another maritime option is through the program known as MARAD provided by the US Maritime Administration. The Mariner Outreach System is a government database of mariners who are willing to help in the event of a national crisis. Registering for the program is simple and comes with no obligation and if a crisis happens, you will be called to help move ships out of port and will be able evacuate that way.

Third, you can escape by air. This is the least likely option for you if you are escaping at the same time as everyone else. Unless you own and can fly your own plane, air transport is going to be prioritized for critical individuals and persons with disabilities. You might also be able to afford to charter a plane or a helicopter if the situation is dire enough and you want to get out before the evacuation order is given.

Fourth, you might walk or bike. Granted this is not plan A, but there is a good chance that Los Angeles freeways are going to be deadlocked if there is an evacuation. Depending where you are and where you plan to go, biking or walking may be a faster way out of the city. Your emergency supplies are going to be limited to what you can carry and the risk to your persons is far greater than staying in a vehicle or a in a building.

Besides the different modes of transport, there are several possible directions to head to when evacuating Los Angeles. Depending on the location of the disaster, instructions from government personnel, your location, and other factors that might arise in a disaster, you may want to head Northwest to Santa Barbara, North to Lancaster, East towards Palm Springs, or South leading to San Diego. If you feel that nearby cities will be dangerous or at full occupancy, areas like the Los Padres National Forest or the Santa Rosa and San Jacinto Mountains might be an option to camp at for a few days.

When evacuating, have concrete plans such as where will you get food, gas, and shelter plus backup routes, before heading out. Research five to ten hotels, as far as 200 miles away and write down their contact information and address so you can make plans quickly.

Evacuation Checklist

Just like your family emergency plan, you want an evacuation checklist ready and visible at all times, in the situation when an evacuation order is given.

When you evacuate, make sure to check all of the following:
• Make sure your gas tank is full.
• Listen to your car radio or check the Emergency Management Department's Twitter account for additional information and updates.
• Be sure to have your Go-kit/ Bug-out bag ready.
• Have a clear evacuation route in mind before leaving.
• Notify your neighbors and other family members when you are leaving and where you plan to go.
• Move valuables to inner rooms or upper floors and in a safe, if you have one.
• If it warrants, board up the windows of your home with plywood.
• Turn off lights and unplug any unnecessary appliances.
• Close and lock all windows and doors of your residence.

- Don't forget cell phones. Make sure they are fully charged and you have a car charger.
- Take a checkbook, credit cards and cash with you.
- Be sure that you have flashlights with extra batteries.
- Drive away from your home at a safe speed.

Bug-out Bag

Not only do you want to be prepared for your final destination, but you need to have enough supplies in case you get stuck in traffic for an extended period of time. Your "Go-Kit" or "Bug-out Bag" should include the following:

- Copies of important documents*
- Food and water (three days worth)
- Medications and copies of prescriptions
- Personal hygiene and first aid supplies
- Items such as diapers, formula, or other special food requirements
- Pet carrier, leash, pet food, and pet medication
- Change of clothes and comfortable shoes
- Emergency cash (small bills), checks, and credit cards
- A list of out-of-state contacts
- Solar, hand-crank, or battery-powered flashlight, radio, batteries, spare bulbs, and light sticks
- Manual can opener
- Matches and a lighter
- Pocket knife or multipurpose tool
- Whistle
- Gloves
- Heavy plastic garbage bags for tarp, poncho, and waste
- 200-pound test nylon line
- Blanket or sleeping bag
- Local maps
- Something to block the sun from your car windows in slow traffic

*Details about important documents
- Driver's license or photo identification
- Passport
- Deeds, titles, marriage license, and birth certificates
- Insurance information and policies
- Most recent tax returns
- Social security cards
- Government programs or services information and eligibility documents
- Will
- Family photos, including service animals and household pets

Evacuating Tsunamis

For tsunami related evacuations, here are the three areas that are most prone and their evacuation routes. A recent study from the University of Alaska Fairbanks looked at how a 9.1 quake off the coast of Alaska could send high waters to California, damaging harbors, especially the ones in Los Angeles and Long Beach.

<u>West Los Angeles Evacuation Route</u>

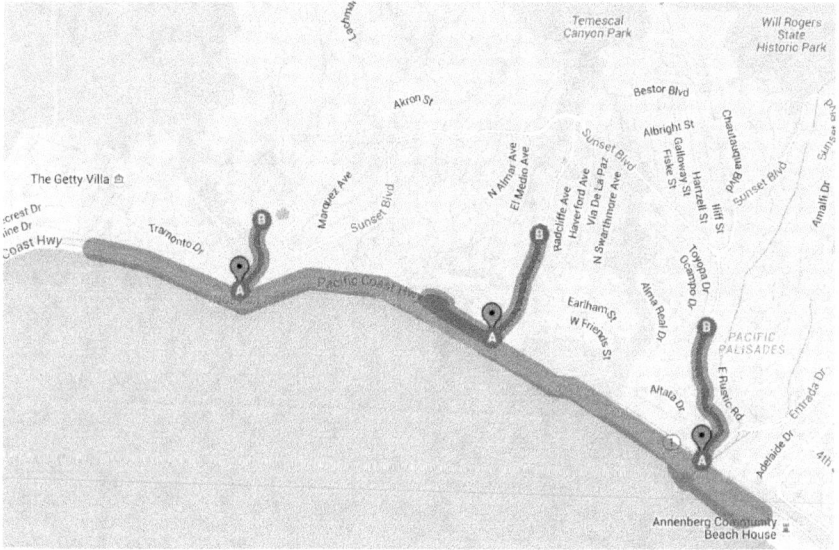

<u>Los Angeles Harbor</u>

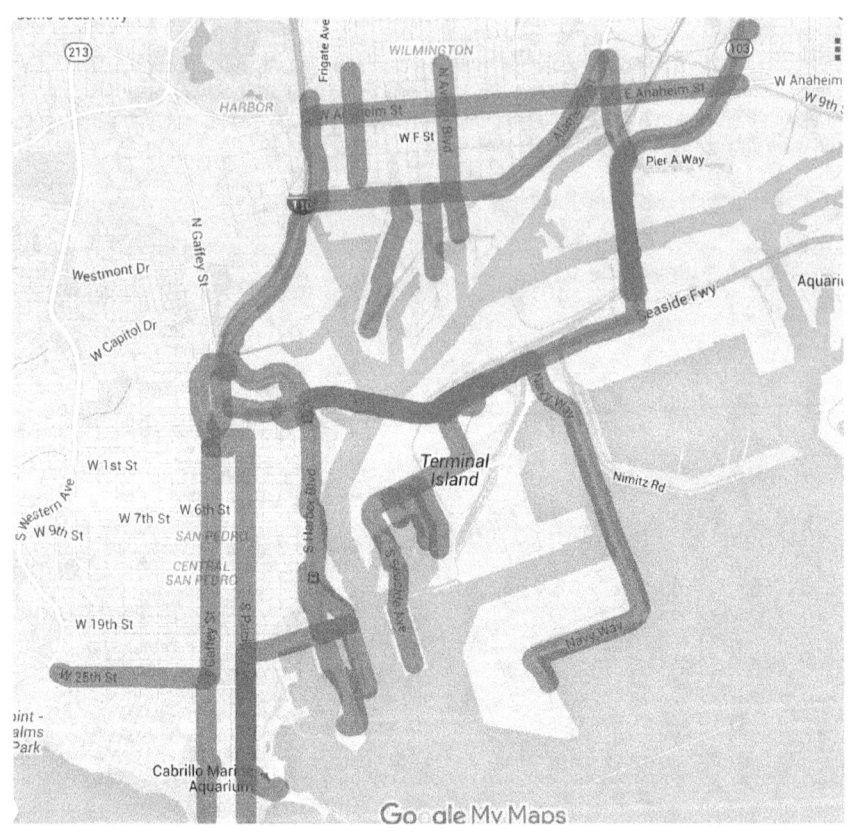

Venice Beach

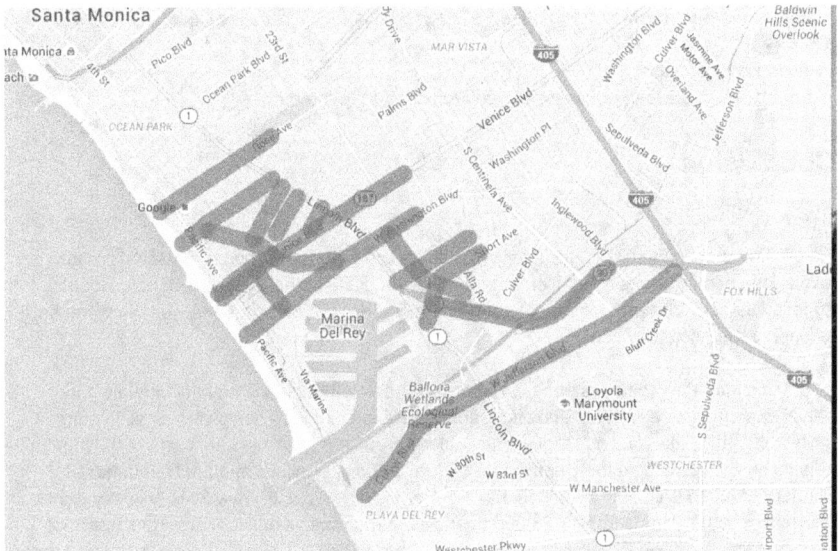

Evacuation for Individuals With Disabilities

       The State of California has placed great emphasis on emergency planning for people with disabilities and others with access and functional needs with the establishment of the Cal EMA Office for Access and Functional Needs (OAFN). Nursing homes, hospitals, and other medical institutions have systems with the local government in an event of an evacuation. If you know someone with a disability that lives at home, have them register with SNAP (Specific Needs Awareness Planning) to make sure that they are cared for during in emergency. Nearly 9% of people in Los Angeles have a disability and it is our responsibility to take care of those who can't take of themselves in times of disaster.

Stuck On The Road

       As I mentioned at the beginning of the chapter, being stuck on the road in traffic during an evacuation is one of the worst places to be. Either evacuating before, finding another route, or staying put in your home are all better scenarios than locked in with tens of thousands of other people who are starting to run out of supplies.

If you find yourself in this unfortunate situation, here are some things you can do
• Make friends with people around your car
• Stay with your car, unless the situation is life-threatening. If your life's in danger then abandon your vehicle.
• Turn off the car when not in use

• Look for restaurants, malls, and other buildings with potential resources that are near the highway
• Ration water and food
• Turn off any duplicate / unnecessary electronics to save the battery

Conclusion

After a Disaster

The emotional toll of a disaster from the loss of a business, home, personal property or loved ones can be devastating. Common emotions include irritability, anger, fatigue, loss of appetite, inability to sleep, nightmares, prolonged sadness, headaches, nausea, an increase in alcohol or drug consumption.

It's important to take steps to promote your own physical and emotional healing by healthy eating, rest, exercise, relaxation, and meditation. Besides using your existing support groups of family, friends, and religious institutions, you may need help from one of the human service agencies such as the Department of Public Social Services and the Department of Mental Health. In LA County you can dial 2-1-1 or visit the website www.211LACounty.org for information and referrals to over 28,000 agencies and organizations that provide assistance such as food, water and shelter after disasters. This service is available 24 hours a day, seven days a week.

In certain extreme cases, you may need longer and more support for food, water, and shelter. You may become eligible for Disaster Assistance from the Red Cross and FEMA. They will attempt to provide housing, medical care, food and water, and other basic necessities after a major disaster strikes.

If you are separated from your family, the Red Cross Safe and Well website is a great tool to use. You can click "List Myself as Safe and Well", enter your address and phone number, and select any of the standard message options. Safe and Well is available 24 hours a day, 365 days a year and is accessible in both English and Spanish.

The Importance of Communities

Research done by political scientist Daniel Aldrich showed that government aid is not the principal way most people survive during and after a disaster. While government assistance is helpful, most emergency responders take far too long to get to the disaster area. Instead, it is the relationships among members of a community that determine survival during a disaster and recovery in its aftermath. He found that people who had been more involved in their local communities, used their personal relationships to stay abreast of relevant information and to get support and aid were the ones most likely to survive a disaster.

Setting up neighborhood networks like Neighborhood Watch and CERT can help you be better prepared for any disaster. Trusting the people around your home is going to give you a huge peace of mind when you need their help the most. Neighbors, not professional first responders, typically perform 70% of all rescues in major disasters, so it's best to be prepared.

When organizing your neighborhood for any kind of disaster, here are some things to consider:
• Care for pets, children, the elderly, and people with mobility problems or disabilities.
• Turn off utilities when a neighbor is absent.
• Take Community Emergency Response Team (CERT) training.
• Learn First Aid and CPR.
• Become a HAM Radio Operator
• Learn about the resources in your neighborhood including skill sets, medical equipment, supplies, and other resources that would be shared in an emergency.

Information on CERT

As a volunteer of the Los Angeles CERT Program, I feel that this book wouldn't be complete without a section devoted to the organization.

The Community Emergency Response Team Program trains residents on disaster preparedness and the hazards that may impact their area. You learn basic disaster response skills, such as team organization, fire safety, search and rescue, and disaster medical responses. Most importantly, CERT members are encouraged to support and supplement first responders by becoming leaders in emergency preparedness in their community. I highly encourage my readers to check with their local Fire and Sheriff's Department's websites to see when the next classes begin. There's no cost, and it's a great way to protect yourself, your family, and your neighborhood.

Vital Locations

Airports:
- Los Angeles International Airport (LAX)
- LA/Ontario International Airport (ONT)
- Bob Hope Airport (BUR)
- Long Beach Airport (LGB)
- John Wayne Airport (SNA)
- Whiteman Airport (WHP)

Ports:
- Port of Los Angeles
- Port of Long Beach

Other Transportation
- Amtrak Station (800 N. Alameda St.)

Hospitals
- Ace Hospice Inc (628 N Vermont Ave)

- City of Angeles Medical Center (1711 West Temple Street)
- Hobart Manor Hospice (1942 South Hobart)
- Keck Hospital of USC (1500 San Pablo St)
- Los Angeles Community Hospital (4081 E Olympic Blvd)
- Metropolitan Improvement Health Center (4904 Crenshaw Blvd)
- Pacific Alliance Medical Center (531 West College St.)
- Saint Vincent Medical Center (2131 W 3rd St.)
- The Village Major House (3860 Crenshaw Blvd)

Interviews

I'm so excited to share this next section with you. The following interviews are from conversations I had with leading experts in the disaster preparation field who have unique insight into Los Angeles specific disasters. I hope you learn as much as I did from these experts. Enjoy!

Professor Dr. Jonathan P Stewart From the University of California Los Angeles (UCLA)

1) What is your estimation of the risk of a 7.0 or higher earthquake in the next 10 years?

We usually estimate these probabilities over slightly larger time horizons. It is very high. Details here: http://pubs.usgs.gov/fs/2015/3009/

2) How prepared is Los Angeles for a major earthquake?

We've made great strides, but have a long way to go. Bridges and hospitals have been improved markedly since the 1994 Northridge earthquakes. Mayor has taken steps to strengthen our most vulnerable buildings (wood, tuck-under parking; older concrete), and these improvements will play out over time. A stable water supply is a big issue, especially given the problems in the Delta and the fault crossings of all the aqueducts bringing water to southern California.

3) What recommendations would you give to residents of Los Angeles to best prepare for an earthquake?

Store sufficient water for your family for 1-2 weeks. Make sure mudsills bolted to the foundation. Brace cripple walls. Brace hot water heaters to walls. Learn drop cover and hold on (http://www.shakeout.org/dropcoverholdon/).

4) Where would be the best / worst place to be in Los Angeles during a major earthquake?

Worst: In an older, vulnerable building
Best: In a modern, properly engineered building

Professor Ertugrul Taciroglu from the University of California

1) What is your estimate of the risk of a 7.0 or higher earthquake striking around Los Angeles in the next 30 years?

Adequately detailed, yet succinct, answers to that question may be found in this short document. https://pubs.usgs.gov/fs/2015/3009/pdf/fs2015-3009.pdf

2) What do you consider the biggest risks in terms of city infrastructure during an earthquake?

Possibly the water and power distribution systems and transportation networks. If you have no power, no water, and no roads for first responders to get to where you are, you will be in trouble.

3) After an earthquake, how do you recommend people stay safe around damaged buildings?

They should simply stay away from buildings until they are cleared by first responders and engineers.

4) Is there anything else you'd like to share with my readers?

The best way to survive earthquakes is to be prepared long before they happen, as they will surely happen, eventually. This includes personal preparation, such as preparing earthquake kits and reading about earthquake safety from documents such as https://www.fema.gov/media-library-data/1421937886237-e683b4975c2c324b18967ead20336b2f/FEMAB526_2014.pdf

There is something arguably more important, however. As a society, we should invest more in understanding and quantifying our exposure against potential earthquake losses and devising innovative ways to improve our resiliency.

This includes funding research in structural and geotechnical engineering and seismology. Research will enable us to understand, quantitatively, the highest risks to our assets, and society in general. This, in turn, will enable us to prioritize our investments.
If we don't invest in seismic safety, we will not be safe by being lucky somehow! This much is guaranteed.

Tom Martin Founder of the American Prepper Network

1) Can you tell me more about The American Prepper's Five Principles of Preparedness?

The principles of preparedness are what's needed for an individual to become self-reliant, independent and prepared for virtually any disaster. Without these principles an individual would tend to be dependent on other people for their needs and unable to fend for themselves should that assistance cease.

2) In your opinion, why do some people prepare for disasters while others don't?

Those who prepare prefer to minimize and mitigate the effects of disasters on themselves and their families. Those who do not prepare have a normalcy bias that leads them to think that "it won't happen to them" or the believe that the government will rescue them in the event of a disaster

3) If you were in Los Angeles, what disaster would you be most worried about and why?
Earthquakes. Water shortages. Civil unrest. In that order. Earthquakes are the most common disaster threat in the LA area. Water shortages are very likely especially due to the dry desert nature of southern California and the droughts Civil unrest because of the dense population.

4) What would you recommend people do to be mentally prepared for a disaster?

Get physically prepared, have a kit, and have a plan. Doing that will give them a much better peace of mind to not panic a major disaster.

5) Is there anything else you'd like to share with my readers?

Start out with FEMA's recommendation by getting a 72 hour kit. The next goal should be to have 3 weeks of essential storage. Then prepare for 3 months. Have an ultimate goal of having a year supply and then learn sustainable living skills

Resources

Below is a list of organizations and their respected websites to check out to best prepare for any disaster in the greater Los Angeles area. They provide great information, communities to join, and alerts to subscribe to. This list is by no means exhaustive, but it should be a great start in having the resources you need at your fingertips.

The Prepper's Urban Survival Website: www.urbanprepperguide.com
Google Plus: https://plus.google.com/102271917180581870090
Twitter: https://twitter.com/CityPrepperPlan
Facebook: https://www.facebook.com/The-Preppers-Urban-Survival-Guide-140050986438508/

Los Angeles Emergency Management Department - http://emergency.lacity.org/
Ready LA - http://www.readyla.org/
LA County Emergency Program - https://www.lacounty.gov/emergency
County of Los Angeles Emergency Survival Guide -
http://lacoa.org/pdf/emergencysurvivalguide-lowres.pdf
LA Emergency Preparedness and Response Program - http://publichealth.lacounty.gov/eprp/
Los Angeles Emergency Survival Program - http://www.espfocus.org/
Specific Needs Disaster Voluntary Registry -
https://snap.lacounty.gov/index.cfm?fuseaction=app.registryLogin&CFID=1578779&CFTOKEN=

25921b1db50b4de9-B7C39A25-0E4F-F55A-F96D0EE66CF9D83D
Alert LA County Emergency Mass Notification System -
http://www.lacounty.gov/emergency/alert-la/
5 Steps to Neighborhood Preparedness - http://5steps.la/
CERT-LA - http://www.cert-la.com/
The Emergency Network of Los Angeles - http://enla.org/
Disaster Preparedness for Pets -
http://www.lacoa.org/PDF/HazardsandThreats/Disaster%20Preparedness/PET%20PREPARED
NESS%20WEB%20RESOURCES.pdf
State of California Governor's Office of Emergency Services - http://www.caloes.ca.gov/
Evacuation Routes (North Los Angeles County) -
https://dpw.lacounty.gov/dsg/DisasterRoutes/map/disaster_rdm-North.pdf
Evacuation Routes (South Los Angeles County) -
https://dpw.lacounty.gov/dsg/DisasterRoutes/map/disaster_rdm-South.pdf

Thank you

Thank you so much for purchasing and reading this book. You should now have the knowledge to prepare for any Los Angeles disaster situation. Always remember that disasters can strike at any time and to always be prepared. Review the book every other year, make plans with your family, and sign up for alerts, so you always know when disasters are happening.

Please Leave a Review

As an independent author, I rely on my readers to post positive reviews on Amazon. Your experience with my ebook is very important to me and I encourage you to share your thoughts for everyone to see.

Step 1: Go to Amazon and search for the book "The Prepper's Urban Survival Guide to Los Angeles"
Step 2: At the top there is a star rating along with the number of customer reviews. Click on "customer review".
Step 3: Click on "Create your own review" and follow the rest of Amazon's instructions. Your positive review would truly mean a lot to me.

Thank you and if for any reason you are not happy with your purchase, please send me an email at ybinstock at gmail dot com and I will send you a full refund.